Illuminations

A Book of Poetry

By

Joseph S. Hertzler

ISBN: 1-4107-5297-6 (e-book)
ISBN: 1-4107-5298-4 (Paperback)

Library of Congress Control Number: 2003093048

This book is printed on acid free paper.

Printed in the United States of America
Bloomington, IN

Edited by Teresa Hertzler Jantz and Julia Hertzler

Cover: Mary's Halo, sculpture by Joseph S. Hertzler
Photograph by Mary K. Hertzler

1stBooks - rev. 10/03/03

Dedication

To Mary, Julia, and Teresa

Table of Contents

ABOUT THE AUTHOR

Nature

Illumination

I believe
therefore
I see

I keep needing
to be reminded
comets
moons and stars
shine
as brightly
at midday
as in a crisp
midnight sky

Gardening Illusions

The garden isn't exactly right
a little off-balance
too crowded
lacking a focal point
perhaps a red Japanese Maple

Gardeners are like that
seeking perfection
of garden and gardener
forever planting and transplanting
over here and over there

Gardening is serious play
mixing onions, parsley and red beets
purple irises and white peonies
assigning periwinkle the task
of smothering out the chickweed

Gardeners are like that
illusions of perfection
looking outward, inward and beyond

If not this season
perhaps the next

Aerated Catacombs

I walk the air

two inches above the frail tilth

listening

as earth worms

build their aerated catacombs

rich castles

of fertile castings

an aid to earth's

thin skin

a mandate to feed

the hungry hordes

Love Affair

I have a perennial love affair with flowers
an on-going dance with perennials
a spring ritual of reproduction
replenishing the world with splashes of rainbow
an amorous display
unashamedly public
inviting bees to feasts of nectar
lifting my spirits with fragrance
to soar with butterfly to yet another spray
I have a love affair with flowers

Cat Claws

Unsheathed
the cat claw-like thorns
guard the long-stemmed
blood-red roses
protection from all predators
except persistent admirers

Dandelions

You parachute your off spring
across manicured lawns
giving the breeze
an easy day's work
Hang-gliding above all earthly care
you show no partiality to
landing sites of rich or poor

On breezeless days
you charm innocent children
to forward your sinister plot to rule the world
they close their eyes and blow
your lightweight geodesic domes
to kingdom come
so you can reign in yet another fiefdom

With lion's teeth
you tenaciously bite the earth
Deep-rooted, permanent resident
more apt to be at home than current occupant
Despised, defamed, decapitated weekly
you recover to raise your golden head
quickly aging into grey before next mowing

to send another generation of invaders

to populate one more lawn

assuring perpetuity

More than a survivalist

you conquer

Flags Of Fortitude

Although fragile
with one day life expectancy
daylilies do not easily die
and I am their witness

having unceremoniously
uprooted tenacious clumps
grabbing grass green hair
to toss at random
down the river bank
toward the setting sun
to land feet first
with a resounding thud

only to find next spring
the west slope
waves with burnt-orange
flags of fortitude

The Red Hibiscus

A simple exchange
a question
an answer
shaped by a philosophy
uncomplicated by the clutter
of knowing more and more
about less and less
an unconscious protest
against trivial pursuit

    Sir, could you tell me
    the name of this flower?

The care-taker
with Myrtle Beach
hospitality
replies

    No sir
    I couldn't
    I could
    but I don't need to know

Lunar Reflector

Giant reflector

are you

servant of the sun

a mirror

saying nothing more

than said to you

echoing back our dreams verbatim

a whisper in semi-darkness

By some mystical power

are you guardian of earth's

night-time

her shadow side

and mine

Within-Without

To conjure up a space
a room which flows into another
an invitation to explore
beyond the back door
an outward-inward place
which stretches
from River Birch to Red Oak
a tall terrarium
wild grapes forming
a canopy of their own
topping the White Pine
and here and there
beneath my feet
an undomesticated flower
the blue flax
a sculpted columbine
self-seeding
like the undaunted dandelion
anchoring earth
and sky

Walking on Clouds

Viewed through the double paned portals
of a pressurized fuselage
walking on clouds
seemed entirely feasible

When the wing
sliced through the whiteness
folding the misty sheets aside
without even a tremor of turbulence
the spell was broken

Would walking on water
be easier?

Leveling

Spring fog, intermediary
between cold and hot
gently airbrushes the landscape
weathered grey
equalizing unkempt weed patch
and manicured lawn

Winter snow, equal parts
of glacier ice
and frosted feathers
throws white blankets
across bedded terrain
smothering differences
between opulence
and the ordinary

And, all that spring fog
or winter snow fails
to impartially level
death will accomplish

Fireflies

Ours is an on-again
off-again relationship
now you light up
and now you don't
Granted, nothing in life
is permanent
yet why so fleeting
so momentary?

I admit
split-second sparks
are better than
no sparks at all
intriguing mystery
drawing me to you
exciting the twilight air
the first evening star

Who can explain
enzymal attraction
heatless light
brightening the night
an invitation to
companionship

Anticipatory Lessons

Hearing a mosquito
circling my head
I began to twitch
and itch
I imagined a welt
back of my neck
a pain
stabbed my left shoulder blade
What power this flying needle possesses
communication in flight
without even alighting
master teacher
of anticipation

And punctuation
Ouch!

Arthritic Farm House

Having stood stiff-kneed
braced against the elements
one hundred forty-seven years
the weathered farm house
like an arthritic elephant
kneels down
kneels down and rolls over
dusting her back
finally ridding herself
of parasites

Deer Tracks

Three deer symmetrically poised
beside Route 20
flawlessly stationed
with head erect sniffing
the west wind for danger
wild sculptured magnificence
I decided to take
all three sculptures
indelibly etched in my memory
home with me
and place them in my garden
near the vineyard
or under
the grandfather sugar maple
or better still beneath
the gnarled Yellow Transparent
apple tree
where deer tracks
mysteriously appear
each Spring

Disrobing

Each autumn
the blushing cheeks of the sumac
give the stately oak
permission to
disrobe

Frozen

The sun was beginning
to penetrate the morning haze
when I saw him sitting
without the buoyancy of boat
as though defying gravity
upon the surface of the pond
frosting the air with every breath
seeking warmth in bulky clothes
disconnected from the world above
oblivious to the world around
peering downward between his knees
in communication with the world beneath
luring miniature dragons to his lair
a throwback to primeval years
the ice age
frozen in time

O Taste And See

She blows
her frosty breath skyward
tasting the temperature
taking several steps
and plumes the air again
greeting the scattered snowflakes
her eye following
an individual flake
the gentle descent
from slated sky
    to frozen earth
        pausing with open palms
            mouth ovaling in awe
the tip of her tongue
searching

To Back Into Joy

Every winter a darkness
a kind of depression
like thick pea soup
trying to suffocate my spirit

The frost is already
blackening the autumn yellow
along with the last light
of white impatiens
while canna lilies beg digging
an alternative to turning into mush

Nights accelerate the assault
days wheeze with shortness of breath
leaving dark upon darkness
the longed-for offer of myriad stars
a nova-like gathering of galaxies
a multitude of angels
singing

The Tree

Which tree
of all the trees
which the knowledge
to know with certainty
the good, the evil

Some say apple, others orange
I vote persimmon

You've seen the type
astringent personalities
shortcutters
exam cheaters rushing forward
for cap and gown
without knowing the tree
the fruit

Premature persimmon pickers
I name them
with tearful eyes
cheeks puckering inwardly
attempting to spit white cotton

Not enough time
to wait the sweet communion
of tree-ripe truth

The Next Generation

I tenderly touch
the top of trees
before Spring spurts
their growth
beyond my
reach

Family

Collective Memory

A piece of the collective memory
belongs to me
the right to interpret
beyond the historian's claim
to eminent domain
beyond the bellicose anecdotes
of mighty military maneuvers
the proclamations
of political potentates

A sliver of history
belongs to me
a deeper stream of reality
of faith and family
an ordinary rooted tree
largely unknown
and unheralded

A piece of collective memory
belongs to me

Delivered

I was born puny
nearly fitting into a shoe box
rocked by Mother
in April's life-giving sun
a substitute for costly vitamins
the year
nineteen thirty-two

I was delivered
at a neighbor's home
next to the deep ditch
draining into Dismal Swamp
the midwife's services
free or nearly so
maybe a mason jar or two
of sauerkraut
flavored with ham

The black earth
sour
crying out for lime

I, too, was malnourished
tenth in a line of eleven
six surviving early childhood

a devoted family
nourishing peace convictions
running counter to country

I was delivered

The Blessing

White-bearded he rocked
oak rasping oak
the faint smell of spearmint
escaping his coat pocket
attracting children
like the pied piper

Seasoned sage sleep-rocking
a lifetime of knowing
grandchildren gliding Indian quiet
across the porch
playing tag under the maples
boundless energy

Rousing, he looked the future
in the eye, saying
    I believe little Joe Joe
    will amount to something

Going on Seven

Such a small memory
easily forgotten you would think
brothers battling brothers for supremacy
the only weapon handy
on the unfenced open range
a wealth of cow pies
hardened brick-like
by the Florida kiln of July

The signal to cease and desist
eludes me as I stoop
to replenish my ammunition
and consequently father's back-hand
sets my left ear ringing

Sometimes on a sultry summer evening
when the wind is hardly murmuring
I think I hear it still

Choosing Up Sides

What looked like child's play
in choosing up sides for kick ball
during recess or dodge ball
on Sunday afternoon
was really serious business
Being chosen first or second
sent a message
to a developing self-ego
different from being
the thirteenth choice
who meanwhile was trying
to act nonchalantly uninterested
as though it was of
no consequence
We all knew it mattered
(but winning mattered more
or so the team captains thought)
and so those less agile physically
sought to develop their self worth
stumbling forward as best they could
Eventually a teacher or two
studied developmental psychology
and chose the thirteenth choices
to choose up sides
giving unprecedented power
to fragile self-images
growing into adulthood

In Preparation

A two gallon can of kerosene
weighs heavy walking home
from the country store
leaning away from the weight
repeatedly changing arms
A raw potato keeps
the kerosene from sloshing
out the spout
    Only grown-up boys
    can windmill filled cans overhead
    without spilling a drop
Saturday afternoon
is time to fill each lamp
trim the wicks
clean smoked globes
and sweep down sooty cobwebs
in preparation
for the day of rest
the Lord's Day
The orange-yellow light
circling the lamp
forces our family to crowd
close together to read
do homework
patch the frayed knees

of overalls
Bedtime isn't far away
Were it not for
the pitcher pump
wash basin
and lava soap
the oily taste and smell
of kerosene would still
hang in the air

Hertzlers and Shenks

I suppose
when you marry late
there is this desperate urge
to redeem the time
the replenish-the-earth syndrome

like Asa and Rebecca
which is how I arrived
next to last – malnourished
certainly not white trash
since dad was college educated
and mom a preacher's daughter

try plain and poor and God-fearing
with two sets of twins
succumbing before
or on the day of birthing
leaving seven
soon to be reduced

to six hungry minds
the living to give the only
testimony of who
they might have been
a new configuration
of the Hertzler nose

another Shenk chorister

to lead a cappella singing

and who's to know - perhaps

a deacon-preacher-bishop

combination

Names On Loan

My mother
Rebecca Susanna Shenk Hertzler Buskirk
outlived her maiden name
two husbands
and most of her peers
Toward life's end she needed help
remembering names of closest friends,
even family

Perhaps that's why
names are carved in granite
with epitaphs
to aid failing memories
Even granite's memory
crumbles in due time

Names and reputations
guarded for a lifetime
on loan from one generation
to the next
the next

Dictionaries

Dictionaries are laborious
bulky books
a grand invention
but a poor substitute
for a father
who already knew
how to spell
all the important words
in the world
and then some
Asking is easier
than paging through the p's
looking for purple
or people
for a third grade
homework assignment
My world suddenly changed
for father finally balked
when asked to spell
the same word
a dozen times
within thirty-six hours
So if I've heard it once
I've heard it a thousand times
"Look it up in the dictionary"

Travel

The porch rocked with her
as did the philosophical afternoon
Traffic, a solid stream northward
sought Michigan's shores
the Mackinac Island
the Upper Peninsula

while the audience
on the porch continued rocking
wondering where
all the traffic came from
and where in such a hurry
all the people were going

And who's to say who traveled farthest
the weathered porch
the rocking chair
or my mother

Crustaceans

Grandfather's lane
paved with oyster shells
recently tonged from the muddy
soul of the Warwick River
still smells of tides

Crustaceans, like bones
give structure to growth
while childhood memories
of bare feet slashed on oyster beds
blood and salt water mixed
warn one to walk reverently

on oyster shell lanes
and ancestors' graves
trusting the calcified
structures of the past
to sweetly lime the soil
of successive generations

Conquering the Eel

With frying pan, bait
hook, line and sinker
three optimistic boys
equipped with sharpened pocket knives
matches, pliers and courage
with backs toward Lucas Creek Bridge
marched west across reedy marsh
to muddy tide
ready to subdue
the salt water eel
    brother to the fish
    sister to the snake
Fortified with salty stories
which twist and turn
tangling the lines
of even the most experienced
who often cut bait and tackle
rather than try to untangle
the slimy scavenger
of mucky depths
from hook, line, hand and wrist
only to find that skinning
was another matter
like peeling off
winter's underwear grown

accustomed to every

shape and bend of your body

but conquered swiftly

once nailed through head

to tree

with pliers to aid the undressing

ready for smoke, fire and sizzle

in Huck Finn style

    we are not dependent

    on grown folks to cook

    our meals

Then why did the first bite

stick in my throat

refusing to swallow

though swallow I must

or endure a life-time

of humiliation

Of Sound Mind

I will travel lightly
across the inevitable Jordan
no excessively weighted luggage
not a single Samsonite
suitcase

I will travel lightly
knowing my abbreviated holdings
my last will and testament will read
being of sound mind...I spent it...
I spent it all

With more exactitude
traveling lightly might best
be described as lights-on living
to be alive
as long as there is breath

I will travel lightly

Maturity

Growing, growing
going, going, gone
a momentary wink or nod
I lost my bid for permanent possession
as well I should
and gained an adult

Anticipation

Insulated beneath the snow
spring gains momentum
tulips wait grudgingly
while daffodils stir the frozen earth
forsythia's budding arms
wave goodbye to wintry arctic blasts

The crocus competes with spring's snowdrops
eager to make the first announcement
and lily of the valley pips
converse among themselves
of June weddings
already in the making

Pomp and Circumstance

White wedding gowns
are ten percent silk and lace
fifteen percent ritual
twenty-five percent anticipation
and fifty percent memories
a small price to pay
for a moment in time
filling an album
with photographs

From One Foot

The Saint Vitus dance
a kind of slang
not knowing
the real medical definition
dancing from one foot
to the other
knees pressed tightly together
not able to wait any longer

too young
unable to unbutton
or button up

delayed maturity
eventually reaching independence
only to return
to the former state
impatiently waiting for assistance
to clasp cummerbunds
and insert cuff-links
starched collars
and shirt studs
demanding the dexterity
of Houdini
a small price to pay
for a daughter's wedding

Nativity

Unclothed
six pound
four ounces
a wiggle worm

with strong voice
letting the world know
of her arrival

arms and legs whirlwinding
like Don Quixote

how could Cristina know
two grandmas
and two grandpas
rather advanced in age
were simultaneously born
when she took
her first
breath

and was christened
Cristina Janelle Jantz

Julia

My daughter is a falcon
an American Kestrel
stylishly dressed in brownish red
with white and black patterned face
Long before she was ready
to leave the nest she flew
hovering over the earth
riding the wind currents
with agile beauty
She still outsmarts
her earthbound prey
devouring lesser creatures: crickets
grasshoppers and mice
without losing her petite profile
Gliding over the landscape
her watchful eye
is aware of the slightest movement
My falcon daughter
is a friend of the clouds
she soars above the ordinary

Tardy Amendment

How can I make amends
for pitting parent-truth
against a child's imagination
confronting my five year old
who kept declaring
she could fly...really fly
insisting on a demonstration
launched in broad daylight
from the front porch
steps

Dignity Intact

Backing her way
toward the mailbox
to collect the morning mail
wearing dirty coveralls
and an impish grin
not willing to give the neighbors
the frontal view of a gardener
covered with God's good earth

the labor of potato digging
on hands and knees

Full-Length

Contented lying lengthwise
across the sagging couch
a full five hundred miles south
to the northern lakes
I hear the distinct call
of the so-called Common Loon
a quaint message traveling
the water's surface
carrying the starched image
of black and white correctness
the ecological barometer
of pristine wilderness
only to realize the plaintive sound
is
at this very moment
generated close to home
the involuntary wheezing
a high-pitched nasal wildness
the rhythm of inhaling
exhaling

Open Window

Sounds
pour through
the bedroom window
open to the low crooning
the mourning doves
staking their claim
on the early morning

Robins
join the chorus
anticipating the daybreak
busy chatter

Trains
pull their cargo
whistling at each crossroad
rhythmically dragging their clacking
toward the horizon

Downstairs
the grandfather clock
counts upward toward breakfast
while beside me
Mary whistles in and out
a gentle snore

Loneliness

When Mary is away
a kind of regression
sets in replacing
habitual routines

The bed doesn't make its self
nor the dishes wash
Teeth-brushing isn't as urgent
and punctuality becomes secondary

One cereal bowl
rinsed out in the sink
suffices for an entire week

Call it separation mourning
a glitch in the forward progress
of civilization
rituals of loneliness

Read Me Like A Book

She can read me like a book
not a complicated mystery novel
I admit
nor a Shakespearean drama
rather a transparent children's story
with a predictable story-line
no need for many words
the pictures tell the story
body language reveals the thought
the echoing footsteps portray the mood
as obvious as a clear stream
like a translucent shrimp with each
heartbeat showing
a one-cell paramecium
under a microscope
with each hair-like cilia
swimming

Thursday's Ritual

One way to measure the week
is to mark off Thursdays
as garbage pick-up day
I like one-can Thursdays
but usually Thursdays
are a can and a half
you know, stuff like
plastic milk jugs
and oat bran cereal boxes

Special holidays are measured
with two full garbage cans
and spring cleaning invariably
swells the ritualistic cleansings
to four garbage cans
and two cardboard boxes
filled with an assortment of items
not even Goodwill or
the Salvation Army will accept

Sometime I absent-mindedly
forget Thursday
and garbage accumulates
leaving me feeling constipated
or not quite clean

after I've showered
I wonder if the town dump
favors heavy holidays
when there is more than
enough to eat
or prefers slim nondescript days
when the earth rests

Thursday is the day
to measure

Making Do

My father-in-law made do all his life
welding, patching, repairing, stretching
as far as humanly possible
When the corn-picker and combine gave out
they were stored in the shed
expecting rejuvenation or resurrection
whichever came first
Given neither they were moved out back
against the day when dismantled parts
might keep other machinery running

Antiquity finally forced farm auction
breaking up housekeeping
leaving a brown grocery bag half-full
of assorted lengths of string
unknotted and neatly balled
each piece a connection with the past
a package from relatives in Ohio
a distributor cap sent parcel post
for the Ford-Ferguson
each string a remnant
of a generation unlearned
in the convenience of throwing
things away and buying new
They call it making do

ingenuously using what's at hand
a lost art in this generation
except for those who substitute
grey duct-tape for bailing wire

Nursing homes remove the necessity
the life-long habit
of making do
forcing father-in-law to improvise
saving table napkins
served three times daily
a luxury unusual on the farm
leaving four brown grocery bags
of slightly used napkins
to the next generation

Blue Mason Jars

Mementos in hazy blue jars
accumulations in musty dresser drawers
prized possessions, time-tarnished
    dangling key chains
    a mug stacked with pencils, erasers hardened
    ball-point pens dry as an Arizona desert
    an unused World War II sugar coupon
        only I can redeem
    seven worn Indian-head pennies
    a battered two-cent piece
    a bag of swirling glass marbles
        reminders of sweaty competition
    an often lost and found pocket knife

Memorabilia losing
its memory

Collapsing Upward

Two gnarled grandparents

like the sagging barn
and wood-stave silo

lean heavily
each on the other

forestalling the day
of dust to dust

collapsing upward

Religious

God So Loved the World

In warm embrace God cradles the world
like a child hugging a prized possession
like a mother cradling her child
like the father in Jesus' parable welcoming back
his lost son with a ring of acceptance
like the Creator who declares
behold, it is very good

A Modest Proposal For Peace

The dovecote's
pecking order
deals gently
with
the loser

Domestic doves
in every home
a lullaby of peace

The Loft

The aviary
housing the domesticated Ring-neck doves
reminds me of a flock
of peaceful pacifists

they seem to know
the wire mesh
is not so much for
keeping in as keeping out

though given a crack
some are known to bolt
thinking freedom is safe
unaware of the hovering

Red-tailed Hawk

Maneuvering Room

Shopping for the right-sized hunting jacket
seems simple enough though doubly difficult
for this violence-abhorring pacifist

An army surplus jacket would never do

Much better an L.L. Bean sports coat
with bulging pockets
bulky enough to give one's conscience
room aplenty to maneuver

Kudzu

A man named Kurtz
or was it Kratz
decides to travel the countryside
to plant the green seeds
of the kinetic kudzu vine
around the perimeters
of a thousand southern military bases

Kurtz or Kratz know's kudzu
has been known to leap tall buildings
in a single season
Being a naturalist he knows kudzu
a legume
replenishes the soil with nitrogen
Its hairy leaves produce oxygen
and eat air pollution
while camouflaging every object in sight
easily able to envelope
an entire battalion of jeeps and tanks
in twenty-four hours
should they turn their backs

Preliminary reports already find
military brass raising white flags
at two hundred thirty-seven bases

claiming these closings
will strengthen military might
an effort to hide the real truth
behind the gobbledygook of double-speak

The expert camouflagers
out-camouflaged by Kurtz's or Kratz's kudzu
proliferating while the troops
are involved in Desert Storm
cover entire military camps
in deep jungle green
Even the troops
equipped with eerie gas masks
and yellow night vision can not
locate their barracks and consequently
return to their homes
joining the civilian population again

PS: I will be eternally grateful
to Kurtz or Kratz for finding
peaceful employment for kudzu
In 1947 my father planted this prolific vine
on our backyard river bank
One Saturday afternoon the unruly kudzu
jumped the fence, climbing the neighbor's trees
blocking out the sunlight
thus creating an atmosphere reminiscent
of an Amazonian rain forest

the cause of an eruptive roil

which my father after explanations

of legumes converting atmospheric nitrogen

into user-friendly nitrogen for plants and animals

did not win

Penitence

Who will volunteer to migrate
in penitence
for the sins of Harry S Truman
dressed in radioactive ashes
of Hiroshima and Nagasaki

Or joining a native American
Indian tribe might suffice
sitting cross-legged day and night
smoking a peace pipe until
peace becomes a worldwide habit

Commiseration with the peaceful
poor of Costa Rica
might constitute repentance
and provide a safe haven
from military might and fright

Should northward be desired
the elongated nights and days
of Reykjavik might freeze
the white heat of war
fifty below without firing a shot

Or better choose the postage stamp
sized country of Liechtenstein
whose last living soldier died
several decades ago of old age
no replacements or war taxed needed

Courtly Dove

Submissively
with lowered neck
with billowing throat
the courtly dove
ill-equipped for war
prepares for mating
and peaceful
perpetuity

The Apple

The apple continues to tempt us
McIntosh, Winesap and Golden Grimes
delightful to the eye
sweet, tart, crisp
heady apple cider
intoxicating

School children
by pure coincidence
offer apples to their teachers
shortcuts to enlightenment

The real tempter is knowledge
learned university chairs
pinnacle of erudition
independent pride

The beguiling serpent played a minor role
seducing our gardening parents

The obsession of knowledge
the hunger to know good and evil
to be God-like
put the apple core under the desk chair
Apples give us

floor to ceiling libraries

wordy knowledge

and sophomoric wisdom

And everyday new apple varieties

are being grafted to hardy

rootstock

Agreement

Listening intently
eyes closed in deep meditation
the sermon drones on
nodding agreement
more than intended
head dropping forward
in slow jerks

The benediction
brings whiplash

Ourselves Too Seriously

We've got it near perfect
staring down those
who think otherwise

Tight-lipped
with few problems
except those easily cured
with an over-night laxative
taking great comfort
knowing little
will need to change
in the New Jerusalem

Out Of Wedlock: 1948

Conspicuously absent she cowers
before the congregation
Only seventeen and found
to be in the womanly way

The air is electric with second guessing:
who took advantage of her willingness
if indeed willing she was?
By rights, if he was any man at all
he'd step forward and offer marriage
Perhaps he should be forced
but it is hard to coerce a wallflower
who has faded anonymously into the woodwork

Ranking sins which cannot be explicitly described
in a mixed congregational meeting
requires a host of innuendoes
with corollary connections to the
unpardonable sin
accompanied by tears of repentance
behavior of a meek and contrite heart

Could it be…premeditating thieves and murderers
who become gloriously saved
from a life of debauchery

are more readily received into fellowship

than a teenager caught in

an unplanned hour of sexual passion?

prompting my father

who thought to bring objectivity and justice

to the meeting by the insertion

of an ill-advised Biblical story

He rose to his feet, cleared his throat

and asked: Now let's see

    Jesus was conceived

    out of wedlock

    wasn't he?

Jesus Judiciously Jumps

Jesus judiciously jumps
over dead-end questions

leapfrogs pharisaic quizzes
designed to play the crowds

hurtles tantalizing taunts
traps for the gullible

pole-vaults over underhanded
inquiries of James and John

Jesus judiciously sidesteps
the questions of this poem

Untitled

Untitled
and unplagiarized
the following lyrical expression
with scalpel precision
single handedly exposes
the shadow side of pacifism
purposely to punctuate pride inflated
the restoration of humility

Doves defecate also

To Ricochet Heavenward

O God, Let Death Take
My Enemies by Surprise
Psalms 55:15

The Psalmist
had no way to know
church business meetings
are the place to get vindictive
not prayer meetings

My father could have told the Psalmist
so many a tension filled session
high pitched voices
ricocheting off walls, ceilings
and closed minds

At times like these the moderator
declares three simple words
    Let us pray
And pray we did

Coordination honed by practice
we swivel out of benches
drop to our knees
face the pew

in three seconds flat

A low homogenized murmur

seeps heavenward

quieting frayed nerves

with layers of memorized platitudes

we, the enemy, taken by surprise

Their Lot

These stalwart women
mandated to mother the world
pastors' wives
a slip of paper found in a book
on the communion table
transforming their lives
and their husbands'
for evermore

A goodly number
having done their best
found they could no longer
sing the songs of Zion
though they kept trying
they began to choke
almost like bearded catfish gulping
for air in the muddy creek
on a blistering day in July
their gills clogged with algae

Having no other alternative
they sought solitude
in bedrooms with windows darkened
staring at the blank ceiling
too weary to pray

their voices remain silent
like the Trumpeter Swan
hiding in the reeds during
molting season

In due time
they emerged on the wings
of the congregation's prayers
and the whispered words
    nervous breakdown
are never uttered
again

Applied Theology

Reverend Taylor, a lay preacher
kept a sharp eye
for discarded copper wire
aluminum castings, scrap iron
and anything metal piled out back
He paid two dollars for worn-out
car batteries
Intermingled with junk talk
a natural flow of parables
simple stuff like

    You take a tater
    planted in the ground
    dirt over it, dirt under it
    dirt all around it
    Dig that tater up
    cut it open
    ain't no dirt in it

    Just like us Christians
    living in a world of sin
    Sin on every hand
    but ain't no sin in'um

I'll give you fifteen dollars
and haul away that rusting
heap of junk out back
overtaken with weeds

    You hook a fish
    lived all its life
    in the salty brine
    put it on the table
    you gotta put salt on it

    Just like us Christians
    Sins all around us…

Loading a dead battery
on his battered red truck
I bait him

    Bet you can make a parable
    on just about anything

Without pausing he said

    Now you take this old truck
    hauled many a load of scrap iron
    its tires got some life left in them
    engine uses only a quart of oil
    for each tank full

body is going to hold together
five or six more years
if I'm lucky
but if she ain't got spark
she ain't going nowhere

Just like us Christians
can't get up and go without
the spark of the spirit...

In Joseph's Carpenter Shop

In tune with out-of-tuneness
the wood rasp
the chiseled parings of the adze
and Jesus
like my father
singing off-key

Unless
like Mary Oyer
or his mother Mary
he had perfect pitch

Lord, Is It I

Somewhere buried in my memory
lies a gray-green busybody
She eats the subjects of intercession
while praying for their salvation
a stick-like praying mantis
who lifts folded
hands

Tough Pacifists

What toy maker
will manufacture
tough pacifists
two inches tall
armed with principle and truth
ready to fight for
the minds and loyalty
of children
against tin soldiers
armed with nothing
but brute force
and firepower

Slow Death

Needles and pins
eight penny nails
railroad spikes
there are several ways
to be nailed to a tree
each unique
as though first-tried

How humiliating
to be transfixed
against the sky
with a thousand pin pricks
dying without
a mortal wound

Petty Sins

Thistles prick
Thorns reach out and grab
Porcupines are said to
throw their quills
The picadors of matadors
pierce the necks of charging bulls
and saints think to conquer the world
armed with faith
with hope
and peccadilloes

Continuity

The wild mulberry stump
springs to life each May
try as I will to prevent it
Haphazardly planted
    or should I say providentially
by an unnamed bird
    perhaps a well-fed robin
in my otherwise orderly vineyard
to teach me to commune
with what was
and is
and will be
continuity with the past
and future
    a root out of dry ground
tenaciously holding on to life
seen and unseen
above and below
before and after
    Jesse's stump

Sweet Revenge:

Seventy Times Seven

The savage adage of eye for eye
of tooth for tooth is
the recipe for a sightless society
a toothless mouthful
begging to give, to receive mutilation

an entire population eating grits
a diet of water and cornbread crusts
unable to gum their way through prime rib
or read statements of justice without squinting

like military brass and prison wardens
the self-righteous claim twenty-twenty vision
the ability to eat beef-jerky without swallowing

who then is left to incarcerate
who left to count
three times you're out

throw away the keys

The Other Side

We are not easily netted
our frantic struggle throughout the night
reddens the water
With brilliant morning light
we cast our nets on the other side
and catch a glimpse of the church's sail
the tree of life
a new vocation

The Quiet In The Land

The vocal extroverts among us
encourage the rest of us
to speak out
share our faith
toot our own horn
so to speak

what do they know
about the inner workings
of our mind and heart

We smile when outsiders
attracted by our genuine walk
and modest talk
challenge us to shout
from the rooftops

Flamboyant preaching is best
left to TV evangelists
who are prone
to trip themselves up
by many words
and extravagant living

come quietly
and we will learn from you
and you from us

Ask Them

The eager evangelical
asks the
broad-brimmed
black-hatted
purple-shirted
black-suspendered
barn-doored
blue-overalled
farmer rocking
in the willowed chair
at Yoder's Department Store
in Shipshewana
the theological question
"Are you saved?"

Without hesitation
pencil in hand
he writes down ten names,
friends, neighbors
and a so-called enemy
or two
and in reply said
"Ask them"

Endangered Species

Scattered across Indian territories
named Shipshewana, Topeka and Nappanee
Amish named Miller, Yoder and Stoltzfus
break ground each spring
behind muscular plow-horses
as did their forbears and mine
dressed in antique blue and black

I gaze enamored as the pages
of history live and breathe
gentle folks turning the earth
in tune with the seasons
Had they arrived in time
with latch strings out
history would have been
savvy barnyard horse talk
smoking peace pipes
without long braids or bowl-cut
hair dangling from warrior's belt
the disappearance of
the Potawatomi tribe

The lilting names of Shipshewana
Topeka and Nappanee
along with an occasional arrowhead

are scant reminders leaving

Stoltzfus, Yoder and Miller

to multiply from farm to farm

despite land prices and interest rates

fueled by modernity

though subsequent historians

may record

the lethal stares

of tourists

more deadly than scalping

A Quiet Testimony

Honor to whom honor is due

In black-brimmed hat
and barn-doored britches
he stands awkwardly
piling cantaloupes
according to size
in cannonball pyramids
beside the road
a cash crop
transported ten miles
by horse and buggy

Already tasting
the home-grown juicy slices
I make conversation
asking the obvious

    Did you grow
    these muskmelons?

Without hesitation he replies

    No, I only planted them
I only planted them

Pregnant Silence

Nothing particular on my mind
an ideal time to write
about nothing in particular
an honorable tradition

Nothingness seems a throwback
to pre-creation running counter
to God and higher education

So why is nothingness eagerly
sought by mystics and sages?
more easily attained by some than others

An emptiness, a kind of waiting
unlike the fill-in-the-time waiting for God
a concentrated nothingness
silence pregnant with expectancy
God's extended hand almost reaching

The Seer

To see
to really see
the primordial sea

a picture
of what was
and is
and is to come

a suction
which plants sandy feet
between the earth and sky
a single wave washing

washing

Cheek To Cheek

Standing their ground
`they shoot the other's heart

    You create your own heaven
    your rewards here and now
countered by
    There is only one entrance
    into the Celestial City

They part friends of sorts
as far apart as east to west
as down to up

    For your sake I would hope
    there is no hell

    And I would hope for yours
    there is a heaven

Twelve Disciples

What a great world

this will be

when our children

play with toys

of the twelve disciples

and fantasize

about a life

of daring adventure

following Jesus

instead of playing

with twelve tin

soldiers

Peripheral Vision

Moses understands
blindness comes quickly
to those who dare
look straight
into God's face

so perhaps

the brilliant colors
of painters and poets
should be savored
with sideward glances
running

Remembrances

Captain Jack And A Hundred Swamp Cats

Captain Jack was one of the last salty fishermen
living in a dilapidated one room shack
in the tidewater marsh
on the shore of the Warwick River
which flowed
(depending on the rising or falling tide)
into or out of
the James River and the Chesapeake Bay

The Captain's face was weathered
from decades of wind, rain and sun
not to mention a life
of debauchery and sin
just the kind of unsavory character
which holds a scary fascination
for ten-year-old boys
who dare and double dare each other
to sneak through oozing marshes
infested with deadly cottonmouth water moccasins
to get a peek of the Captain's shack
or perhaps the Captain himself

A skilled salt water fisherman
Captain Jack rowed his boat
across inlets and coves feathering his oars
without sound or rippling wake
Wild cats swarmed around his shack

at twilight when he gutted the day's catch
fighting over fish heads and stringy guts
with nothing uneaten except a million
fish scales bouncing eerie reflections
back at the moon

One story told with calloused relish
by the Captain sticks in my memory
true or false I will never know
>   After a long day fishing
>   I returned to my shack dead-tired
>   hung my cap and coat on the nail
>   by the door, I did
>   and was sound asleep
>   before I hit my bed
>   During the night I was awakened
>   by a terrible noise
>   grabbed my loaded rifle
>   and fired in the direction of the ruckus
>   Dead silence
>   I rolled over and immediately dropped
>   off to sleep not knowing if I had
>   killed the intruder or not
>   At the crack of dawn I awoke
>   to find a bullet hole
>   smack in the middle of the forehead
>   of my cap hanging
>   at a man's height by the door
>   I shoot first and ask questions later
>   Here let me show you my cap

The Captain also said he didn't need
bed covers even on the coldest nights
His pillow was a big black cat
weighing forty pounds
The other cats piled on three deep
making the warmest blanket of genuine fur
in the whole world
(but that's another story)

For some unimaginable reason
parents weren't keen about
their children hanging around
Captain Jack's shack
but he mellowed with age
coupled with the influence
of a straight-laced church goer
who saw beyond his rough exterior
and wild tales

When the Captain died
he was given a Christian funeral

Who Is To Know

I can't remember whether Denbigh
my home of birth
left me or I left her
who is to say who left whom

The only barn still standing needs strong arms
to travel across the field
leaving the magic moments of spring calving
and real dirt farming behind

Peach orchards are squared off into subdivisions now
no longer dropping bruised fruit to satisfy
hungry children and thirsty wasps

The precipitous dip in the road
by what was Colony Farm Dairy
no longer swallows cars for breath-holding seconds
and Burkholder Dairy has long since been sucked dry
with only a lingering scent of skim milk

The parochial school cellar
carefully dug beneath the Warwick River Church
is no longer worried about collapse
since the remains are buried near the cemetery
Although Newport News has jealously claimed the terrain

Denbigh will remain along with the muddy Lucas Creek
and the Warwick River tiding in and out
I'm convinced that some will remember

Artistry

As a chicken dresser Aunt Dora

was lightning fast, an artist in her own right

She was old, plumpish, about forty-five

I was young, energetic and fourteen

Determined to be the best that I could be

I whetted my knife stroke for stroke

with Aunt Dora (a sharp knife is the key to speed)

and tried to ignore the heavy stench

of blood, wet chicken feathers and high humidity

I concentrated, studied her every move

Aunt Dora didn't seem to concentrate

She chatted about this or that

and that and this

while circling the rectum with surgical precision

She opened the body cavity

extracted the entrails taking special precautions

with the greenish gallbladder filled with bitter bile

lest it burst upon the liver making it inedible

Skillfully she split the slippery gizzard

without cutting its lining

and extracted is gritty contents intact

She rescued the heart and discarded the crop

Aunt Dora was nearly finished

She rinsed her bird

and plumped it in scalding water

to tighten the skin into a taut healthy glow
She deftly reached for a second chicken
while I was pulling entrails
hand over fist from my first
When finally I triumphantly plumped my bird
Aunt Dora was plumping her third
    Three to one - artist and butcher
    One to three - butcher and artist

Aunt Dora is obsolete today
automation has seen to that
but after sixty odd years
I still admire artistry
no matter the medium

Ten Years Old And Growing

Around the bend
just east of Kraus'
hiding in the thick water
of the Lucas Creek
is easy
Clinging to the muddy bottom
like tidewater crabs
moving sideways
lungs finally aching for air
bursting the surface
with mouths gaping open
gasping for air
like a giant hippopotamus

Staying under too long
worries the others
the game of hide and seek
can go too far
and leave a chum hidden forever
in the sucking swamp mud

Relieved as the last swimmer breaks
surface we fling fists full of oozing mud
at each other
black war paint lying on the bank

until the warming sun

bakes a mud crust

from head to liberated toe

unaware we are

naked

Non-Smoking: 1944

Dried apple leaves

rolled in tissue paper

during recess

were a poor

substitute for tobacco

but were enough

when word mysteriously reached

Mrs. Carper

(the parochial school principal)

to merit a belting

in front of the fifth grade class

and a life-time

ban on smoking

Goatburgers

Leading a goat to the slaughter
isn't difficult
Slaughtering is another matter

Intent on supplying nourishment
for a growing family
Paul Sauder selected a baseball bat
as slaughter weapon
without understanding the anatomy
of a goat's skull which is ten times
harder than a wooden bat

He swung as though intending
to hit a homerun
The sickening thud shook
this twelve-year-old bystander
to his toes
The yearling goat rolled its eyes
staggered
bellowed a mournful baa
but stubbornly refused to fall or die
    I had seen and heard enough
    too much and left

The next day during school lunch

Bill Sauder (my age) generously
offered me half a sandwich
of freshly butchered goat meat
while describing how he quickly
ran to the toolbox
    to shorten the suffering
and got a ballpeen hammer
so his father could
knock the goat out cold
before cutting its throat

Gingerly holding the goat meat sandwich
I quickly reviewed my options
not sure if I could stomach
or keep stomached
the sights and sounds of yesterday
As I hesitated momentarily
Dan Nice or was it Wally Schaefer
unencumbered with goat acquaintances
asked "aren't you going to eat that"
while snatching it from me
and scarfing it down
before I could offer a weak protest

I still wonder: does goat meat taste
more like mutton or beef

Less Than Humane

The Humane Society
is more likely to prosecute
Lewis Burkholder, Johnny Shenk
and Johnny Garnand
who fifty years ago
were stalking the jet-black scavengers
(If they didn't do it they
will remember who did)
gifted glider of air currents
ungainly on the ground
made bold by hunger
noisily gorging themselves
on the heifer carcass
awaiting burial in the ravine
back pasture behind Burkholder Dairy

Capturing one ghoulish vulture
they meant to place him
not themselves
in harm's way
tying a stick of dusty red
tree-stump dynamite to its left leg

Burdened with deadly cargo
akin to the Stealth Bomber

bouncing the runway

becoming airborne with difficulty

circling back directly over head

seeking an upward air current

causing one unnamed fearless

though unharmed braggart

seeking nonexistent cover

in open pasture or desert sand

to crap his pants

Who will expand the charter

of the strangely named Humane Society

beyond the vulnerable elongated necks

the piercing eyes and pointed beaks

of turkey buzzards and cormorants

to strident shouts protesting

the harpooning of hapless Iraqis

like fish in a water barrel

The dynamite's detonation deafens

ear drums

vaporizes the hapless bird

Not even a wing feather

a fingernail

or a prayer

drifts to the sand

Swear Not At All

Nobody in my growing up group
said the d___ word
at least out loud
much less the s___ word

We were country church folk
and swearing was accepted
as sinful although slang words
such as Gosh and John Brown
were tolerated though not encouraged
Taking the Lord's name didn't even
exist in our subconscious minds
Extra adjectives weren't necessary
The ideal was:
    Let your yea be yea
    and your nay nay

Consequently on a sleepy
Sunday afternoon Twila's parents
relocated in the dining room
to clear the living room
for twelve teenagers
to wile away the hours
playing sanitized table games
when D_____ dropped the s___ word

quietly but with intensity
like pent-up steam driven
through a pin hole
louder than the seven trumpets
in Revelation
and blacker than the fourth
apocalyptic plague
there was silence in heaven
for twenty four hours
echoing off the ceiling and walls
assaulting our ears and
numbing our brains so that no
quick retrieve from mortification
was possible

We all knew the social etiquette
code had been violated and
perhaps a gross and grievous sin committed
and since one swear word leads
inevitably to another
would it not lead eventually
to the unpardonable sin

The fear of total ostracization
forced Daniel and myself to form
Swearers' Anonymous
The rules were quite simple
though urgency compelled us to

fix a five cent fine for every

unnecessary adjective

that inadvertently passed our lips

We must have exchanged a thousand

nickels but the fear of poverty

strengthened our willpower

and heaven rejoiced

Judge Not

In my eager drive
to excel
I showed disdain
for Josh Carpenter
who stood around
staring into outer space
through unsheathed roof rafters
picking his nose
waiting for step by step
instructions before
breaking trance
clearly unfit timber
for framing crew
menial labor

He married good
earned an advanced degree
in counseling
developed social graces

I continue to pick
at this and that

Mulberry Island: 1945

Conquering the choppy Warwick River
a mile wide at age thirteen
was no mean achievement
given occasional salty whitecaps
and the tugging out-going tide
making it necessary to aim northwest
to land on a parallel point
or find yourself
foundering in the James River
heading for the Chesapeake Bay

Conquering the River was uneventful
compared to mysterious Mulberry Island
surreptitiously confiscated
with words like eminent domain
and national security
the last vestiges of homesteads
long since obliterated
by tangled walls of honeysuckle vines
and the silent invasion of kudzu

The intrigue of the Island
apart from being a true island
only when high tide
a full moon
and a strong south-easterner coincided
was, you weren't supposed to go there

The military needed practice
and practice they did on land
by air and sea
though the latter was unintentional

The rattling rat-a tat rat-a-tat a-tat-tat-tat
filled my head and the belly of Mulberry Island
with enough lead to poison
the ground water for a thousand years
or until the Lord returns
whichever comes first
kept me from conquering the Island
the falling bombs flashed the sunlight

seldom hitting intended targets
each bomb filled with a wheelbarrow of sand
and a cup of dynamite
enough to plume the watery Warwick
sixty feet skyward
and burst a water main six feet under
on the mainland missing Mulberry
by a wide mile

The military almost stifled me
although I swam the long mile
to her shore without touching bottom

Principle and determination kept me afloat

not allowing me to wade the shallows

finding out years later the tide

flowing in and out was borrowed

to flush the personal raw residue

of Fort Eustes

past the indiscriminate beds of oysters

toward the open sea

The Bell Ringer

yet unborn—
a bright hope
in the womb of potentiality

The raw energy
a wild hope
his face set toward a valley
of drought
the porous dryness
of bleached bones
an Ezekiel-like daring
of hope against hope

not a half-wish
sun-blessed picnic
but rather a bone-marrow
persistence
like the out-of-work
William and Mary president
ringing the frozen college bell
every day
without students
without faculty or dollars
to send out the clarion call
finally heard
seven long years after
the whitening bones
of the uncivil
Civil War

Frontal Attack

Retired engineer George McCormick
dressed in bib overall and railroad cap
He was a large man built like a train
His bulbous nose gave hint
of a train headlight shining in the dark
George was always on the go, a floor pacer
Chewing tobacco was his favorite past-time
though his aim was poor (or so I thought)
The floor around the spittoons stained chocolate
and the Angel-wing begonias and Snake Plants
at the end of the hall by the barred windows
thrived from the ingredients of tobacco spit
Hardening of the arteries
was the official reason for committal
(or did they say syphilis was the culprit)?
Pacing the halls of Western State Hospital
George searched for the Baltimore and Ohio station
and when nature called - the toilet
When he began to fumble to unfasten
so he could drop his bib overalls
experience taught me he was in search
of the latter
In moments like these timing was everything
Bold action was called for
I sprang into motion
grabbed George's broad shoulders

but in my haste I found we were standing
face to face

I began to turn him south
toward the toilet but he, quicker than I
responded with neither understanding
nor gratitude
hitting me full in the face
with an enormous mouthful
of concentrated tobacco juice
blinding me completely
My eyes burned
as though stung by a thousand bees
Shooting stars burst in the darkness
Stumbling into the wall
I felt my way down the hallway
past a dozen doors
to the archway and turned left into the toilet
I remembered the urinals were on the left
so I veered right groping my way
to the sink
Oh, the joy of cool pure water

Then and there this do-gooder vowed
to forego future face-to-face
frontal attacks
no matter the circumstance

Cornered

Following the war
when meat was rationed
    except poultry and fish
at close of market day
a customer asked
for a fryer
Reaching into his tub of ice
the butcher pulled out
his last chicken
Too thin and light-skinned
she said
    most customers preferred
    the brownish skin of Rhode Island Reds
    to the pale epidermis of White Leghorns

Throwing his lone fryer
back in the tub
he swirled the icy water
and held it up again
for her perusal

That's better she said
Looks healthier
I'll take two

Collective Memories

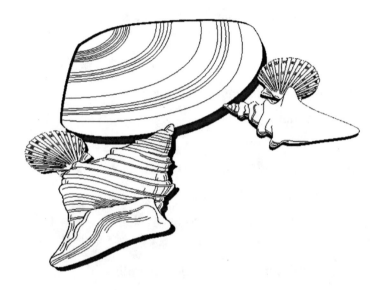

Homemade Jars of Jam

Courting poverty mother and father
could ill afford to give gifts
even inexpensive ones
    Oh, the sadness of survival without giving

At canning time mother and my sisters
used one third the recommended sugar
on bruised fruit
for sugar was too expensive
Nevertheless a few jars of jam were canned
and jealously rationed out at company dinners
    Ah, the luxury of jam at company dinner

When guests ventured the smallest compliment
mother, over protest, insisted the company take
a jar of jam
peach or plum
    Ah, the satisfaction of giving, that is living!

Temporary Cleansing

Moving across the room
four abreast
in a kind of cleaning ritual
aprons and tea-towels
rhythmically waving
driving the circling horde
toward windows propped open
a door slightly ajar

An exorcism of sorts
though never quite complete
Too many holey screens
three corner tears
screen-doors sagging

The flies creep back in
attracted by the sweet and sour
a cat-dish beside the wood-box
leftover milk
peach peels, pits
a mason jar with nicked lip

Four abreast
three women and a boy
move across the room

Riding Toward Home

Home is the place you run to
or can hardly wait to run away from
depending on your need for stability
or your intolerance of rigidity
when you are fourteen

Forced separation is another matter
even though at the point of departure
there was outward agreement

Home is mother singing at the sink
father fencing up his grapes
a house filled with brothers and sisters
so when home itself up and moves
leaving a sibling a thousand miles behind
the gravitational pull
is ten times stronger than the moon
causing a junior adolescent
with nothing but pocket change
the clothes on his back
a spare in a sack
a large bulky Bible
protection from all evil, known and unknown
to secretly start pedaling southward toward home
on a balloon tire one speed bike

After all he was the eldest child
senior of six siblings
and incurably homesick
although several months earlier
it seemed a grown-up decision
to earn his keep
at Aunt Mary and Esther's in Virginia
making one less mouth to feed
while the family got settled
in Florida

He arrived safe and sound
needing a shave
just in time to try and regain
his elder son status
without realizing that a six month
separation changes family patterns
which may account for
running away from home for an Army stint
against the clear convictions
of dad and mom

and fifty years later
may account for
the semi-veiled ambition
to find refuge and shelter in a safe
country farm of the Old Order Amish
protected from worldliness by patriarchal fiat

provided of course they ordained him bishop

Superiority

We lived next door to wealthy folks
who ate store-bought Post Toasties
lived in a painted house
drove a reliable car

Our family ate cornmeal mush for breakfast
a light lunch
fried mush for supper covered with tomato gravy
lived in a substandard house
drove our car when it started
    This was before the invention of jumper cables
    so, when possible, we parked on a slope
    for an easier push start

Our neighbors occasionally gave us food
and from time to time ill-fitting
hand-me-down clothes
as well as advice
on how to get rid of head lice
    dip your head in a kerosene bucket
    but be sure to cover your eyes

Fifty years later and a half dozen states apart
I met our former neighbor's niece
Momentarily I felt she was the one deprived

I paused and began to wonder

what psychology-in-reverse over the past five decades

made me feel superior to my benefactors

Prejudices die slowly

Home Alone

Alvin didn't go along
the rest of the family jumped
into the aged thirty-chevy
scavenging for food
the leftover butter beans hiding
in the field after the harvest

maybe Alvin wasn't feeling good
perhaps he felt leftovers
were above his dignity

not far behind the house
the railroad train mourned
its way across the Florida palmetto brush
lonely tramps walked the tracks
looking hopefully for a handout

Alvin thought to help the deprived
and gave from the scant cupboard
a hefty chunk of cheese
the smooth talker knew who was vulnerable
and ended up using dad's razor

which didn't please the head of the house
so he scalded both the razor
and Alvin

Fiasco in Florida

The laying hens aren't to blame
they didn't build the rickety pen
the possum's empty stomach
growling for giblets
loud midnight cackling wakes
dad and dad senses
breakfast without eggs
and bartering advantages lost
at Sebring's country store

Needing fortification
Alvin the eldest is flushed from sleep
dying flashlight batteries silhouetting
flying feathers and the rat-like
tail of the determined marauder
rusting wire-mesh giving scant protection
the aging outhouse offers roost

Morning light confirms chickens
aren't strong swimmers
the privy lid left open
playing possum unnecessary

Closing the Back Forty Gate

Faster than the evening breeze
the quickening twilight
drives my churning feet
the bamboo-like reeds
throw grotesque shadows
like Dismal Swamp black bears
ready to devour this small boy
in a single bite

forcing me to run the lane's
weedy center, sand-briars and all
my noisy heart sounds like
steps gaining over my left shoulder
and mom, to relieve her worry
sends the rescue squad
my older siblings

meaning no harm
they jump my path
my windpipe gasping great gobs of air
an uncontrollable whooping-cough rasp
the only cure by mother's arms

sometimes on moonless nights
I hear steps gaining

Smelling Out Your Own Kind

Mom lived in mortal fear
the ill smelling Billy goat
with menacing curve of horn
would lose interest trailing
docile nannies
sniffing out their heat
mount the dilapidated fence
cross the road to our yard
and attack one of her children

It tried once and mother counter-attacked
with the only lethal weapon on hand
a common household broom
fearlessly sweeping the stinking brute
off our premises

The smell of its antisocial visit
lingered long after his forced departure
longer still in the porous
broom bristles which remained outdoors
for an extended airing out
which gave ample time
for in-house muttering about
irresponsible neighbors
Billy goat owners with distorted values

class distinctions which
followed to logical conclusion
explains why national enemies
leave a lingering Billy goat stench
for decades

A Strand of Hair

Life may be held together
with a single strand of hair
a precarious tradition
based on a mixture of fact
and fiction, religion and emotion

When college disciplinarians
in 1914 decreed
no bushy chin length sideburns
Dad defiantly complied by shaving
his right sideburn high above his ear
After a lopsided week his classmates
felt siding with the authorities was justified
so hog-tied father pruned
his left sideburn

Following this sophomoric fling
Dad began to take hair seriously
mustaches were off-limits because of
World War I military connotations
GI haircuts of World War II
were taboo

My brother, David
came home with a flat top

Dad chased him around
the kitchen table with a fly swatter
Mom's hair remained untouched
by shears not because of style
but as a statement of faithfulness
to Scriptures and Dad

The strength of hair
should not be underestimated
Samson lived to regret
a hair stylist named Delilah

The Reunion

A thousand experiences
and so little time to share them
Ideas by the score
and the floor already taken
already littered

Three years accumulation
takes a great deal of dumping
I mean to say
sharing

We try taking turns
knowing the gregarious extroverts
among us
will invent new ways
to interrupt mid-sentence
to embellish old stories
to finish incomplete sentences
still in the birthing process

The only defense for the hesitant
a low murmur
another level of conversation
camouflaged beneath the first
a raised eyebrow

Chaos as usual reigns
everyone talking at once
nobody listening

I guess it isn't important
that everything be heard...
just that everything
gets said

Reflections

Self-Sufficiency Short-Lived

I was stubbornly independent
my dependencies exclusively mine
till I realized
that the air I breathed
was manufactured
by a thousand trees
and I could hold my breath
for only
a minute

Amber Night-Lights

Like a parked diesel truck
my brain keeps idling
while my body sleeps

Amber night-lights define the space
the exhaust snores sporadically
ready to transport freewheeling dreams
through a maze of memories
brain-waves traveling faster and farther
than eighteen wheelers
weaving through traffic

A half-closed eye keeps watch
on the rear-view mirror
for the nightmare
of flashing red lights

My brain keeps idling

Insomnia

The night
bent double
crawls past me
leaving me
bleary-eyed
at sunrise

Tension

My stomach muscles
circling
the day's problems
like a hungry
python
slowly squeezing
until no oxygen
remains

Scuffed

I found myself
reaching toward
and smiling foolishly
to no one in particular
standing in front
of a Skoal's tobacco display
mistakenly thinking
the black
brown
tan and white
flat tins of snuff
were wax shoe polish

Both my brown shoes
and composure
were scuffed

Maybe The Mail

No mail today
not a single piece
Perhaps it's a holiday
President's Day or something
Maybe the mail is late
hasn't gone yet
although all my neighbor's
mailbox flags are down

I feel a lonely sadness
No first-class mail
not even an electric bill
a connection of sorts
to humankind
I would be satisfied
with the somewhat
less personal mail
addressed
to the current
occupant

Ca'wd, I Never Have (Chagrined)

The Photograph

She sat framed on his desk
hair pulled back tightly in a bun
straining facial muscles
reminiscent of two decades since

The five and dime frame molding
offers no compliment
prompting a misguided question

> Why don't you get an updated
> picture of your wife?

> *This is a recent picture!*

The Chicken House

The long low roof-line
ties ten apartments together
without distinction
no costly frills, no gables
housing for seminary students

> They look like chicken houses
> to me. I wonder who designed them?

> *I did!" said the architect*
> *standing alongside*

154

The Fair

Hard bleacher benches
loud country music
keeping my distance
the welcome silences
filled with sexist jokes
Leaving early I meet friends
late arrivals
breathless to hear
their favorite singers
    I hope they are better than
    the singing group I just heard
        They are the singers
        we came to hear!

Serious Business

Laughing is serious business
Come laugh with me
beside me
laughing seriously

When laughter eludes me
when humor disappears
laugh for me
in my stead

Laugh with me
beside me
before or after me
below me or far above me
but never
laugh at me
I reserve that right
for myself

Gallows Humor

Without a smidgen of history
my sixtieth birthday present
large splashes of earth-tones
hangs conspicuously
on the closet tie rack
a newcomer among well-worn
knits, stripes, paisleys
and stains of experience

The gasp is audible
The snickers keep spreading

The slip knotted noose
tightens up a notch
asking

    who will hang next
    and who
    next to whom?

Descending

Consider the jar
to your tired aching feet
stepping down from a curb
finding nothing but air

More serious the plight
ascending the throne
with intention to sit
in regal composure
the shock to discover
your dignity's descent
unexpectedly lowered
the seat left upright
by the last
occupant

Winning Without Entering

The odds of winning
the Publisher's Clearing House
sweepstakes
ten million dollars
all for you
are about the same
with or without
a ticket

Avoid Perfection

Forget total recall
avoid perfect pitch
and shy away from high C

jog for the joy of jogging
flee four minute miles

read for the joy of reading
ignore encyclopedias

shun technical definitions

Live the unknown maximum
    Most things worth doing
    are not worth doing right

Ink Thoughts

Sometimes
when I'm not thinking
uninvited Rorschach tests materialize

Take writing-pens
for example
has anyone under oath
been witness to
the death of a ball-point

Perhaps they are commercially
designed dead or alive to accumulate
in cracked coffee mugs
doomed to dehydration
like my grandfather's
brown envelope of black powder
resting on my desk
thirsting to fill
the ink-well

A Seminal Thought

A seminal thought
hurriedly written
on the back of an envelope
or a white folded napkin
yellowed with mustard
might be expanded
in poetic splendor
to rival the masters
I distinctly remember
it's in my shirt pocket
that I wore on Tuesday
or is it stuffed
in my faded jeans
What a loss it would be
to the whole of creation
if that bit of scrap paper
got thrown out with the trash
and in the town dump
be reduced to grey ash

Feedback

You didn't say
what you thought
of the poetry I shared
and you are not obliged
although I had hoped
yet do not need
for you to share
your inmost thoughts
as I shared mine

You hesitated long enough
for me to interrupt
the awkward silence
and keep you as a friend
instead of a reluctant
critic

Double-Jointed

Take this poem
by the tail
and look it
square in the eye

Paper Thoughts

The unwritten page
begs the ball-point pen
to craft a pithy phrase
to justify
the unarmed limbs
the barkless branches
the pulverized heart
of the fallen tree

Even Webster Equivocates

Words
like rowboats
bob about on shimmering lakes

submerged
barnacle-like crustaceans
with serrated teeth
surreptitiously cling
to time-worn meanings
slowing the pace of change

who can hold back
the next generation of poets
with feathered oar
they row toward distant images
merging past with future
watercolors blending
bleeding across the page
unexpectedly

definitions
rocking gently with the waves
continue to drift

even trustworthy
Webster
equivocates

These I Can Do Without

Grit in my spinach salad
eggshell in my omelet
tiny white worms in dark green broccoli
sharp poppy seeds under my lower plate
black pepper in my windpipe
leaking ballpoint pens in my shirt pocket
cold sores on chapped lips
a gnat in my lemonade
yellow egg yolk on my blue necktie
beach-sand between bed sheets
grey cigarette smoke in my eyes
long hangnail on my index finger
limp hair in green split-pea soup
quartz pebble in my left shoe
sunfish bones stuck in my throat
half a worm in an apple
a red pimple on my nose
an itch between my shoulder blades
a mailbox filled with current-occupant mail
gossipers without content
sharp cracking gum in my ear
tailgaters with high-beam lights
water in a skillet of hot oil
red lipstick on three front teeth
mosquitoes on a hot July afternoon

a radio station just out of reach

genuine artificial leather belts

basses who sing falsetto tenor

writers who don't know

when to stop

Bone of Contention

The point is
though you are
bone of my bone
you feel a need
to ask

what is the point

signifying
further discussion
is pointless

unless you

unless we

Glassed In or Out

Window picture
double reflection
is the scenery framed
looking in or looking out?

Translucent boundary
on which side do you stand?
Can so thin a skin of glass
protect you outer or within?

Fragile partition
of melted sand
can an unseen blow
shatter your frail ego?

Invisible wall
even the birds leave
feathery wing prints
narrowly escaping death

Naked protector
letting daylight in
and night-light out
Self-revealing to a fault

Sheer crystal pane
is there nothing left to hide?
Enough self-revelations
let drapery close your eyes

Pinned Down

Pity the small doll

crudely manufactured

with arms

haplessly molded

to its sides

unable to return

a hug

or dream away

childhood

playing patty-cake

except

in make-believe

Unnoticed

She would
have noticed me
had she
realized
    everybody
    is
    somebody

Please Erase Me

Most dreams dreamt
are quickly forgotten
and for good reason

Most thoughts thought
do not merit publication

Most poems concocted
should never be written

So if I am
a dream, a thought or poem
please erase me

Like John Henry

He sledge-hammers
his slanted stakes
sharp-pointed
deep
into every argument

muscles flex
to form
the tilted axis
of his world

like John Henry
the greatest
spike-driver alive
he works alone
his sharp words
skewing all in earshot

Sparring

Digging in deeper
than a striped badger
strategically backing
into its burrow
snarling and snapping
incoherently
at the verbal barrage

a kind of semantic game
of cognitive phrases carefully crafted
impeccable logic
requiring instant recall
and substantiating footnotes
along with mathematical exactitude
with dates and circumstances
a sure way to drive
the slower wit like myself into full retreat
backing downward
into the gaping underground orifice
vowing silence

only to realize later
semantic sparring seldom
changes minds
much less the world

An Ode to Compulsion

To lie or not to lie
the spoken word
the unchaste bed
is hardly the question

the astronomical ability
to shade
to convincingly
shave the truth

but in the end
the grey-green praying mantis
deliberately
eats her mate

Oddly Solitaire

Homo Sapiens

social animals par excellence

hundreds herding together

thousands flocking into football stadiums

identifying with body contact

sitting alone on crowded bleachers

applauding team strength

ten thousand black birds

all talking at once

nobody listening

encouraging two bull moose

loners by nature

pawing the artificial turf

to defend their territory

back and forth

one hundred yards

a kind of group therapy

social solitary

Difficult

Difficult it is
to communicate
eye to eye
to share
to carry the burden
each of the other

Difficult it is
to keep warm
to express intimacy
back to back

To The Aft

Backing up or backing down
is an unnatural state
awkward at best for bulldozers
dump-trucks, politicians
and television evangelists
forcing safety-minded law-makers
to mandate
an obnoxious high-pitched siren
to warn innocent bystanders
standing to the aft

Still Unlearned

As the predator approaches
the wild barnyard cat
frantically eats its newborn
protective instinct
overriding motherhood

Had there been time
she would gently teeth
the nape of each neck
to carry dangling offspring
out of harm's way
    a lesson still unlearned
    in international
    squabbles

Metaphorically Speaking

When bread is more
than a life staple

a cup more than
quenching thirst

when a dove exceeds flight

a rose surpasses
petal and stem
at the moment

and yes my heart is valued
beyond pulsating
pumping

Act Your Age

Popular wisdom to the contrary
and although instructed otherwise
at an early age
I have nevertheless concluded
that people spend their lives
trying not to act their age

As a boy when I pushed or shoved
mother shamed me by admonishing
"act your age"
which being interpreted in hindsight
meant act older than you are
pretend to be mature beyond your years
sit down
be quiet
and do not cross your eyes

Now that I'm older and getting grey
my mother's instructions still ring my ears
I continue to pretend my age is otherwise
My bald spot carefully camouflaged
My dentures genuinely artificial
Fortunately my arthritic limp disappears
en route to the bathroom each morning
I resolve to be younger than I am

So I rest my case
chronological age
is something you
are never supposed to be
unless
perhaps
there are several hours
sometime in mid-life
    which in my case slipped by unnoticed
when being neither young or old
on one sunny afternoon
all pretenses aside
chronological age and behavior
coincide

Mortality

Red Zinnias

To keep a silent vigil
beside the waiting bed
the ruddy red zinnias
cling tenaciously to life
sipping water
intravenously

Nodding heads lift

The inevitable wilt
postponed

Alzheimer's Song Of Silence

"to the strain and flicker of recall"

Moving forward toward silence
forward toward forgetting
experience after experience disappears
hiding
in the secret recesses of the mind

Myriads of memories drifting
freed from the moorings of time and place
an unanchored buoy flickers on and off
moving toward a desolate island
complete thoughts unretrieved and unretrievable

Only the slow rhythmic beat
of primordial waves
the slow sad singing
of Come Ye Disconsolate
calling you back

Calling you back

Thin Oatmeal Mush

The aging brain can gradually
turn to a thin oatmeal mush
with only a raisin or two
of sound judgment left to float about
in brown sugar and skim milk

How else to explain
our saintly mother's
decision to send part
of her social security check
to right-winged Jerry Falwell

or her plaintive request
to the nursing home attendant
to shear her uncut hair
and paint her natural
finger nails bright red

I Need Love

A thin plaintive cry
pale blue
echoed down the corridor
penetrating my bone marrow
thin and pale blue
tasting of loneliness
At first her call
carried a conscious need
a drink, a shawl
to know the time
the day, the year
but time inevitably changes
nursing mothers
to mothers that need nursing
subconsciously calling
Nurse, Nurse!
a universal primeval cry
echoing down nursing home hallways
everywhere
tenuously connected to reality
Nurse, Nurse!
What do you want?
I...I don't know. I want you
(that's partly true)
Nurse, Nurse!

What do you need?
And mother suspended between here
and the hereafter replied
I…well, I need love

Immortality

She dies quickly
four months after hearing
the dreadful word
cancer
though not before
her artistic mind requests
white starched wings
to fill the casket

Uncomforting Comfort

I really do not understand
how God could let this happen
    You certainly don't
    God was the first person present
    sharing the pain of my son's death

We know it was God's will
    No, the fatal accident
    was not God's will
    but we appreciate your concern

God surely must have loved
your daughter so very much
to take her home so soon
    Over there by the casket
    is my ninety-one year old aunt
    God mustn't love her
    much at all

I always say when your time is up
your time is up
    I still think it's wise to look
    both ways before crossing the street

All things work together for good
to them that love the Lord
    Are you sure that includes
    an untimely lingering death
    from cancer?

You'll understand it better by and by
time is the great healer
    Perhaps, perhaps

All Flesh Is Grass

All medical cures
no matter how spectacular
are followed eventually
by the death of the patient
as well as the doctor

The Earth Must Wait

Possessions shrink
with shrinking days
finally all else discarded
to own a single sacred
three by six feet plot
of real estate

The earth must wait
no plans
for immediate occupancy

The Eulogist

The time has come
and none too soon
for a few choice words

a circumspect selection of memories
a kind of verbal dance
skirting the known idiosyncrasies
of the deceased

the dark edge though unspoken
hovers discreetly
between the lines

Instinct

Stymied I stand before the mirror
my razor feeling awkward in my hand
a strange contraption
two thin blades mounted on a handle
part of a wake-up ritual
practiced daily for five decades
momentarily disappearing

Do I ordinarily shave from left to right?
or right to left? From sideburn to chin?

And what's to become of the songbird
who loses the instinct to sing?

llife

GIVING THANKS FOR ALL THINGS

"Praise the Lord"
Sang the Psalmist

"O GIVE THANKS TO THE LORD,
FOR HE IS GOOD;
FOR HIS STEADFAST LOVE
ENDURES FOR EVER!"

Our Father in heaven,
Reveal who you are.
Set the world right;
Do what's best—
as above, so below.
Keep us alive with three square meals.
Keep us forgiven with you and forgiving others.
Keep us safe from ourselves and the world.
You're in charge!
You can do anything you want!
You're ablaze in beauty!
Yes. Yes. Yes.
Amen

MATTHEW 6:9-13
(the message)

Neighborhood Group
COLLEGE MENNONITE CHURCH
FALL 2015

Rapture

Beyond words
inexpressible
Heather, age three
undiluted joy
over-riding speech
stiff-bodied on tip-toes
squeals
top lung capacity
hands wave
like flags wind-whipped
caused by the soft touch
a bundle of white fur
a three-week-old
Netherlands Dwarf rabbit

teaching adults
pure rapture

Connecting Sounds

How unfortunate to live beyond
the long mile
crossed by the crowing rooster
subduing the fence post
declaring himself
in charge of the approaching day
unaware that sprawling suburbia
with citified codes
outlaw his boasting
under the rubric of
barnyard fowl

Ask The Road Runner

The Road Runner knows the limits
of earth, of sky
verbalizing her domain
with brash outcries
a wary eye toward the sailing hawk
while searching for a sleeping lizard
an edible lunch

The paradise of San Diego
seems to forget

    the earth is the Lord's

and continues to embellish the terrain
houses materialize like ten thousand ethereal
poppies coloring California canyons
extending mountain heights
while mansions stilted like circus clowns
taking unsure steps

    unaware the fullness thereof

will bite back
in due time

ask the streaking road runner
she will know the limits

Weather Reporting

Evicting those with prior
land-title isn't easy
natural groundhog habitat
long before my ancestors
sailed the Atlantic

Tunneling their home
intending permanence
beneath the compost pile
east entrance and south exit
hidden by honeysuckle bushes

seeking privacy
receiving short-lived notoriety
the second of February
from so-called
weather analysts

Inherited Space

The stinkbug
alias Hemiptera Pentatomidae
part insect
and part prehistoric dinosaur
moves with deliberate air
wading tank-like
across my kitchen floor
daring me to interfere
owning his own space
and mine

A double-folded paper towel
fails to protect me
from his protective scent
though I'd guess
lightning and lady bugs
will quietly inherit
the earth

Greyhound

The lean greyhound
hunger driven
accelerates

the futile hope
of a belly filled
of rabbit

without realizing
the circling chase
of his own tail holds
more promise
making ends meet

The Weather Vane

How proud the palpitating breast
the swaggering stance
silky white with purple wattles

caretaker of the waking dawn

a lofty latitudinal survey
four corners of the world
single-handedly inventing
the Garden of Eden
again
and
again

Roosters Don't Crow

The Silver Sebrigh bantam
dressed in white
each feather fringed in black
polishes his ivory spurs
watch out world

the first streak of light
and the non-stop crowing begins
the strident shrill throat
penetrates my sleep and beyond
neighbors feign deafness

fortunately I came upon
a motley man dangling two chickens

instead of neck ringing
I politely donate my woes

roosters do not crow
upside down

Rumination

Now I lay me down
to meditate
before I sleep
like a contented cow
pastured out
calmly chewing her cud
cooled by apple tree shade
today's grazing memories
in slow animation
wrapping tongue around
white clover clumps
the wild smell of garlic
smart-weed
dandelion
the prick of thistles
the sweet juice of fallen apple
mouthful after mouthful
ruminating from one stomach
to the next
salivic juices mixed
with the digestive
powers of God
a sleepy salvific
prayer

Ruby-Throated

Airy lightness
like a miniature angel
an unexpected visitation

Hovering wings
a momentary
shaft of light

Ruby-Throated Hummingbird
painting my thoughts
with iridescence

The Starling

Even the starling
has a pleasing
repertoire
of songs

Bravery

The daddy long-legged spider
three inches across
from toe to toe
almost nothing in between
pounced on me
or did it pounce past me
away from me

Unsure, I pounced back
instinctually squashing
the gangly monster
into smithereens
before I could determine
who pounced on whom

Would a purple heart
be appropriate

The Ultimate Insult

Walking the center line
the black-white skunk
paid the supreme sacrifice
lying-in-state five days
road crew irreverence
painting a yellow stripe
down the skunk's back
a mockery to bravery

The Uneasy Truce

The Red-Tailed hawk
with powerful wings
and binocular eyes
mouser par excellence
lies upside down beside Route 57
one wing waving
like a feathered chieftain
in the wind-draft
of each passing vehicle
a grey eighty-three Pontiac
a silver eighteen-wheeler
still not enough upward draft
to perch the top-most branch again
to survey the uneasy truce
of the animate and inanimate
invariably moving in a
collision course

The Monkey Sock

It is time to take a family member
part Lab, part Chow, to the veterinarian
nothing serious, two shots
and a yellow worm pill

While mother is writing the check
the four-year-old daughter
receives some unexpected attention

Doctor Zehr focuses his stethoscope
on her stuffed monkey sock
    Nothing to worry about
    your monkey will be OK
    in a day or two

Out of earshot
the daughter emphatically says
    Mother
    I don't trust that man
    He thought my monkey
    was alive

Gently Stinging

Flight feathers
feather flight
gently lighting on the nest

Those who think
to look
at nestlings beneath
the protecting softness
are greeted by
a flashing wing
the stinging blow
more surprising
than lethal

Doves: A Necessity

"A dove house fill'd with dove and pigeons
Shudders Hell thro' all its regions." William Blake

"Fearfully, we release our doves of peace,
and every time a dove flies back
with hope in her beak, we rejoice." Hough Jr.

What do you do with your doves
I've been asked repeatedly
an innocent question though lacking imagination
limited by experience with obvious pets
like dogs and cats
(no offense meant, no offense taken)
Might as well ask
what do you do with flowers
trees, paintings, goldfish, clouds

A dove is more than its name
more than its shape, its size
more than feathers that fan the air in flight
(as delightful as overcoming gravity so effortlessly is)
Doves are symbols of gentleness
harmlessness, innocence
a statement of contentment and peace
Doves are necessary
The question is
How can you live without doves

About the Author

The author, Joseph Shenk Hertzler, utilized his writing abilities by writing sermons while pastoring in Virginia, Iowa and working at the Associated Mennonite Biblical Seminary (AMBS) in Indiana. Over the years he used his creativity in many art forms including oil painting, gardening, landscaping, sculpture (see front cover), raising many birds including exotic pigeons and peace doves. He participates in a poetry group, affectionately called Dead Poet Society. Joseph is an ordained pastor with his M. Div. He worked at AMBS as vice-president of development for 26 years and is currently retired.

Joseph, fifth of six children, spent his childhood in Newport News, Virginia and central Florida. He is married and has two daughters. He currently resides in Goshen, Indiana.

Printed in the United States
142341LV00001B/291/A